DUETS ARE FUN

BOOK 1

COMPILED, EDITED and ANNOTATED by
DAVID HIRSCHBERG

CONTENTS

Cover Art: Rafael D' Sabino

CLEMENTINE

*Arranged by
Franz Mittler*

Our arranger, Franz Mittler, is a member of the First Piano Quartet. This distinquished ensemble is heard regularly on one of the major networks and makes extensive concert tours.

SECONDO

Allegretto

American Folk Tune

CLEMENTINE

Arranged by
Franz Mittler

This humorous song with its story of Clementine who wore
shoes "number nine" was first introduced in New Orleans
about 1890 in an American Minstrel show. It still retains its
popularity.

PRIMO

American Folk Tune

VOLGA BOAT SONG

Arranged by
Doris L. Crandall

Our arranger, Doris L. Crandall, is a native of California who received much of her training from Homer Simmons. Besides her teaching and composing she has done considerable two piano work.

SECONDO

Russian Folk Tune

Moderato

VOLGA BOAT SONG

*Arranged by
Doris L. Crandall*

Truly the most wonderful of all Russian Folk Songs. It depicts
the Russian boatmen pushing their boats through the muddy
waters of the great Russian stream, the Volga. It is strong and
powerful in rhythm.

PRIMO

Russian Folk Tune

Moderato

M.P. 211-48

ABIDE WITH ME

Arranged by
Adam Garner

Our arranger, Adam Garner, gave his first public concert at six.
At eight he was guest artist with the Philharmonic Orchestra
of Warsaw. He studied under X. Scharwenka (a pupil of Liszt).

Andante   SECONDO   Monk

ABIDE WITH ME

Arranged by
Adam Garner

A frail and ill minister, Henry F. Leyte, wrote the poem which inspired this hymn when he realized that death would soon part him from the sea and the fisherfolk he loved so dearly.

Andante   PRIMO   Monk

SKIP TO MY LOU

Arranged by Vladimir Padwa

Our arranger, Vladimir Padwa, studied at Conservatories in Leningrad, Berlin and Leipsic. He has concertized in Europe, United States, Canada, Mexico, South America, Africa, and the Far East.

SECONDO

American Folk Tune

Gaily

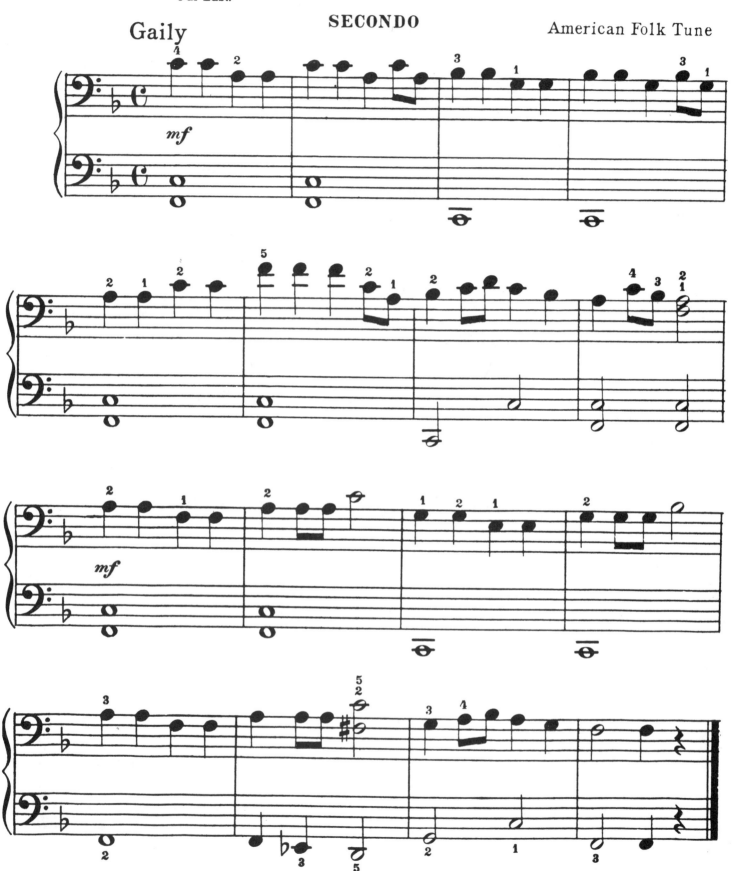

SKIP TO MY LOU

Arranged by
Vladimir Padwa

The old American Square Dances are now going through a re-
vival. This tune was always a great Square Dance tune, even
in the days of the early settlers. Nowadays the trend towards
American Folk Songs has re-established it.

PRIMO

American Folk Tune

E.L. 2510

LULLABY

Arranged by
Franz Mittler

Our arranger, Franz Mittler, arrived in America in 1938 virtually unknown yet in 1939 he had the honor of playing before the late President F. D. Roosevelt at Hyde Park and the White House.

SECONDO

Brahms

LULLABY

*Arranged by
Franz Mittler*

Johannes Brahms composed this enchanting tune. Though he
wrote symphonies, concertos, and other great works yet this
simple little lullaby has made him famous in the hearts of the
people of the world.

PRIMO

Brahms

SILENT NIGHT

Arranged by
Madeleine Spence

Our arranger, Madeleine Spence, is a distinguished concert pianist and teacher of outstanding ability. She has studied at Peabody Conservatory under a Scholarship and there received Teacher's and Pianist's diplomas.

SECONDO

Christmas Song

SILENT NIGHT

Arranged by
Madeleine Spence

This melody of eternal beauty was composed by one who was
not a great composer nor a highly educated musician. He was
a poor teacher in a small school in Austria. Written in 1818
the Christmas bells still ring out its tune.

PRIMO

Christmas Song

Andante

COUNTRY GARDENS

Our arranger, Louis Sugarman, made his debut as a concert pianist in 1929 at Town Hall. He is a composer of many published works including a piano method written in conjunction with the renowned Isidor Philipp.

Arranged by
Louis Sugarman

SECONDO

Old English Dance Tune

Allegro

COUNTRY GARDENS

Arranged by
Louis Sugarman

In the days of King Henry VIII "Morris Dances" were very popular. Many couples standing opposite one another participated. Each couple held a ribbon between them under which the other dancers passed.

PRIMO

Old English Dance Tune

Allegro

OLD BLACK JOE

*Arranged by
Felix Guenther*

Our arranger, Dr. Felix Guenther, is a noted Musicoligist, composer and arranger. He studied at the Vienna Conservatory.
Later he became head of the People's University (Berlin).

Andanté

SECONDO

Foster

OLD BLACK JOE

Arranged by
Felix Guenther

Stephen Foster wrote most of his songs about the South. We all know "OH SUSANNA", "SWANEE RIVER" and "MY OLD KENTUCKY HOME." At one time "OLD BLACK JOE" was Stephen Foster's most popular song.

PRIMO

Foster

E.L. 2510

DARK EYES

Arranged by
Mildred Waldron

Our arranger, Mildred Waldron, teacher, concert pianist and organist graduated with honors from the music department at Wellesley College. Her work as a Music Director has brought her considerable recognition.

SECONDO

Russian Folk Song

Moderato

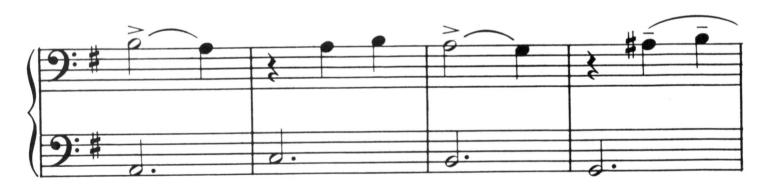

DARK EYES

Arranged by
Mildred Waldron

The Russian gypsies composed many love songs of sad and
haunting beauty. The world has adopted many of these songs
as part of its own heritage. This song is by far the most famous
of all these tunes.

PRIMO

Moderato

Russian Folk Song

NARCISSUS

Arranged by Franz Mittler

Our arranger, Franz Mittler, concert pianist, teacher, composer and arranger at an early age revealed an amazing musical talent. At seven he composed and at thirteen he wrote chamber music works.

SECONDO

Nevin

Allegretto

NARCISSUS

Arranged by
Franz Mittler

This is undoubtedly the most famous piece written by our American Composer, Ethelbert Nevin (1862 - 1901). Though it was originally written for the piano, it is most often heard in its orchestral version on the air.

PRIMO

Nevin

Allegretto

YANKEE DOODLE

*Arranged by
Vladimir Padwa*

Our arranger, Vladimir Padwa, concert pianist, teacher, composer and arranger is a member of the First Piano Quartet, the unique four-piano team well known to American radio and concert audiences.

SECONDO

American Folk Tune

YANKEE DOODLE

Arranged by
Vladimir Padwa

This tune was originally an English melody. The English soldiers, during the Revolutionary War, sung it mockingly at the
Yankees. Later based upon this tune, the American soldiers
made Yankee Doodle their war song.

PRIMO

American Folk Tune

SHORT'NIN' BREAD

Arranged by
Adam Garner

Our arranger, Adam Garner, in his teens played for Paderewski who rewarded him by saying "Some day, my boy, you will be a great artist, and Poland will be proud of you".

SECONDO

Negro Folk Tune

Moderato

SHORT'NIN' BREAD

Arranged by Adam Garner

Here is an American Negro song that is truly different. It is not a Spiritual nor a song of troubles and woes. It is indeed a rarity—a popular negro humorous song.

Moderato   PRIMO   Negro Folk Tune

AMERICAN PATROL

Arranged by
Doris L. Crandall

Our arranger, Doris Crandall, in addition to composing, playing and teaching has varied interests. She loves the outdoors, writes poetry, teaches Sunday School and goes in for cooking, sewing and gardening.

SECONDO

Meacham

Light and lively

AMERICAN PATROL

Arranged by
Doris L. Crandall

This stirring march with its strong patriotic flavor is one of the most popular of all Marches. Its composer, F. W. Meacham, is not otherwise known for any other work.

PRIMO

Meacham

Light and lively

WILLIAM TELL

*Arranged by
Felix Guenther*

Our arranger, Dr. Felix Guenther, noted musicologist has written books on Schubert and Mozart. At present he is a member of the music education staff at the New Haven State Teacher's College.

SECONDO

Rossini

Fast and forceful

p sempre staccato

WILLIAM TELL

Arranged by
Felix Guenther

Though the opera is hardly ever performed yet this melody to
the Overture lives on. This theme depicts the fury of the soldiers rushing to the defense of their beloved country. Nowadays it is a famous radio theme.

PRIMO

Rossini

Fast and forceful

SHEPHERD'S HEY

Arranged by
Franz Mittler

Our arranger, Franz Mittler, owes much of his success to his
sense of humor which enlivens his music. His humorous stories
are delightful and many of his humorous verses have been
published abroad.

SECONDO

English Folk Dance

Allegro

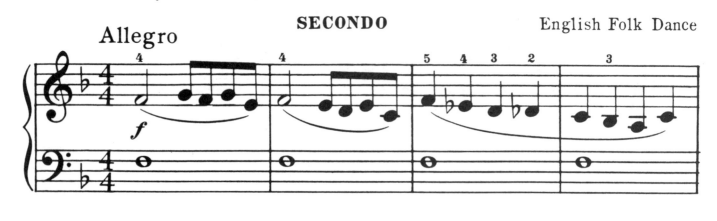

SHEPHERD'S HEY

*Arranged by
Franz Mittler*

The Morris Dances and Sword Dances represent the highest development in the English Folk Dance. They are a survival of primitive fertilization rites and nature ceremonies practiced before the dawn of civilization.

PRIMO

English Folk Dance

ARKANSAS TRAVELER

Arranged by
Louis Sugarman

Our arranger, Louis Sugarman, pianist, teacher and composer
studied with George Copeland, Eleanor Ferguson and for six
years at the Institute of Musical Art with Dr. Percy Goetschius
and George Wedge.

SECONDO

Old American Dance Tune

Allegro

ARKANSAS TRAVELER

Arranged by
Louis Sugarman

First originated more than a hundred years ago in Arkansas,
it has become a universal American favorite. It was first written for the old time American fiddler who never failed to in-
clude it in his repertoire.

PRIMO

Old American Dance Tune

OLD MAC DONALD

Arranged by
Madeleine Spence

Our arranger, Madeleine Spence, had the honor in 1925 of having one of her easy teaching pieces selected for transcription for blind children in Braille.

SECONDO

Old American Humorous Song

Cheerfully

OLD MAC DONALD

Arranged by
Madeleine Spence

This merry tune concerns ducks, turkeys, pigs with their quacks, gobbles, and oinks. Just plain silly—but lots of fun. College students love it—quite naturally! So do we!

PRIMO

Old American Humorous Song

Cheerfully

AMERICA

Arranged by
Vladimir Padwa

Our arranger, Vladimir Padwa, is prominent in the field of chamber music and as an accompanist having been associated with famous artists such as Mischa Elman, Zino Francescatti and others.

SECONDO　　　American National Anthem

Moderato

AMERICA

Arranged by
Vladimir Padwa

This melody is of English origin. The British National Hymn, "God Save the King", is based upon it. The composer is unknown. In 1832 the American version, "America," was first sung in Boston.

PRIMO

American National Anthem

SAILOR'S HORNPIPE

Arranged by
Adam Garner

Our arranger, Adam Garner, distinguished concert pianist, teacher, composer and arranger is a member of the famous First Piano Quartet heard regularly over a nation-wide radio hookup.

SECONDO

Sailor's Dance Tune

Allegro

SAILOR'S HORNPIPE

Arranged by
Adam Garner

The English sailors composed their own tunes for their own merry dances. This amusing melody reflects the unconcerned gaiety so typical of sailors. The dance for this tune is a solo dance with a funny twisting of the body.

Allegro **PRIMO** Sailor's Dance Tune

MERRY FARMER

Arranged by
Franz Mittler

Our arranger, Franz Mittler, has recently devoted his talents to
writing educational piano music for the children of America.
In this field he has won wide acclaim from outstanding teachers
everywhere.

SECONDO

Schumann

MERRY FARMER

Arranged by
Franz Mittler

Robert Schumann wrote many pieces for his children. One of these was "THE MERRY FARMER" One can feel the great joy of the farmer and almost hear him sing this joyful tune while he works.

Schumann

PRIMO

M.P. 211- 48

POLLY WOLLY DOODLE

Arranged by
Bernice Rosner

Our arranger, Bernice Rosner, pianist, composer, teacher and choral director is a Hunter College graduate, who twice was awarded a Lewisohn Music Scholarship. For several years she was assistant supervisor of music in Pontiac, Michigan.

SECONDO

Allegretto

American Folk Tune

POLLY WOLLY DOODLE

Arranged by
Bernice Rosner

This is a true folk tune. Nobody knows who composed it nor where it was first played nor who wrote its words. This we know—that it has lived on and is today loved by all Americans of all ages.

PRIMO

American Folk Tune

Allegretto

AMARYLLIS

Our arranger, Dr. Solomon Pimsleur, has written Oratorios, String Quartets, Trios, Vocal and Operatic Music, etc. His work has been extensively performed by Symphony Orchestras including the New York Philharmonic.

Arranged by
Solomon Pimsleur

SECONDO

King Louis XIII

Grazioso

AMARYLLIS

King Louis XIII of France (1601-1643) who was greatly interested in music composed this. It is a French romance. It's beautiful melody testifies to the fine melodic gift possessed by the King.

Arranged by
Solomon Pimsleur

King Louis XIII

PRIMO

Grazioso

MINUET
from Don Juan

Arranged by
Mildred Waldron

Our arranger, Mildred Waldron, has done extensive musical work in Portland, Oregon. Here she has concertized, taught piano and organ and has been Organist and Musical Director for 15 years at First Unitarian Church.

SECONDO

Mozart

Moderato

MINUET
from Don Juan

Arranged by
Mildred Waldron

This charming tune was composed by Mozart for a scene in his opera, DON JUAN. In this scene persons of high society charmingly danced this minuet inside a Spanish castle.

PRIMO

Moderato

Mozart

Belwin's Keyboard Ensemble Series

The BEST in teaching and performing ensembles

PIANO DUETS (One Piano — Four Hands)

AND IN THE CENTER RING!
(Collection) (EL 03511)
by John Robert Poe

DUET DANCES (Collection)
(EL 03517)
by Mack Wilberg

DUET IMAGES (Collection)
(EL 03484)
by Irina Kirilenko

THREE POEMS, Op. 20 (PA 02283)
by Edward MacDowell
edited by Maurice Hinson

WHAT IF . . . GOPHERS HAD GRANDMAS? (Collection)
(EL 03576)
by John Robert Poe

PIANO TRIOS (One Piano — Six Hands)

AMAZING GRACE (PA 02210)
arranged by Carrie Kraft

BROTHER JOHN (PA 02205)
arranged by Carrie Kraft

CAMPTOWN RACES (PA 02291)
arranged by Carrie Kraft

JESUS LOVES ME (PA 02292)
arranged by Carrie Kraft

MARCH OF THE MICE
(PA 02201)
arranged by Carrie Kraft

MY HAT, IT HAS THREE CORNERS
(PA 02293)
arranged by Carrie Kraft

OH WHERE, OH WHERE
(PA 02206)
arranged by Carrie Kraft

SCARBOROUGH FAIR (PA 02204)
arranged by Carrie Kraft

THIS OLD MAN (PA 02203)
arranged by Carrie Kraft

VALSE AND ROMANCE
(PA 02284)
by Sergei Rachmaninoff
edited by Maurice Hinson

WHAT A BEAUTIFUL SAVIOR
(PA 02207)
arranged by Carrie Kraft

PIANO DUOS (Two Pianos — Four Hands)

AIN'T MISBEHAVIN'
(PA 02312)
by Thomas "Fats" Waller,
Harry Brooks, and Andy Razof
arranged by Heitler/Lyke

ALEXANDER'S RAGTIME BAND
(PA 02286)
by Irving Berlin
arranged by Heitler/Lyke

ALLA TURCA (PA 02332)
by Wolfgang Amadeus Mozart
arranged by Sylvia Rabinof

AMERICA, THE BEAUTIFUL
(PA 02320)
by Samuel A. Ward
arranged by Heitler/Lyke

CHACONNE ON AIR "DIDO'S LAMENT"
(PA 02319)
by Henry Purcell
arranged by Sylvia Rabinof

EVERYBODY'S DOING IT NOW
(PA 02287)
by Irving Berlin
arranged by Heitler/Lyke

THE HAPPY FARMER (PA 02333)
by Robert Schumann
arranged by Sylvia Rabinof

THE HAPPY FARMER AND HIS FAMILY (PA 02318)
by Robert Schumann
arranged by Sylvia Rabinof

INVENTION NO. 8 (F Major)
(PA 02273)
by Johann Sebastian Bach
arranged by Sylvia Rabinof

INVENTION NO. 13 (A Minor)
(PA 02315)
by Johann Sebastian Bach
arranged by Sylvia Rabinof

MUSETTE (PA 02274)
by Johann Sebastian Bach
arranged by Sylvia Rabinof

THE NUTCRACKER SUITE
(PA 02282)
(two copies necessary)
by Peter Ilyich Tschaikowsky
arranged by Nicholas Economou

PATRIOTIC COHAN, a Medley
(PA 02303)
by George M. Cohan
arranged by Heitler/Lyke

POUR LE LUTE (Little Prelude No. 3 in C Minor) (PA 02317)
by Johann Sebastian Bach
arranged by Sylvia Rabinof

SOLFEGGIETTO (PA 02275)
by Carl Philipp Emanuel Bach
arranged by Sylvia Rabinof

THREE FOR TWO (PA 02354)
by Alice Jordan

TWO BACH MINUETS (PA 02272)
by Johann Sebastian Bach
arranged by Sylvia Rabinof

TWO LÄNDLERS (PA 02331)
by Ludwig van Beethoven
and by Franz Schubert
arranged by Sylvia Rabinof

WHEN THE MIDNIGHT CHOO-CHOO LEAVES FOR ALABAM'
(PA 02288)
by Irving Berlin
arranged by Heitler/Lyke

PIANO QUARTETS (Two Pianos — Eight Hands)

ALLEGRO DECISO (PA 02187)
by George Frideric Handel
arranged by Virginia Speiden Carper

BALLOON POP POLKA
(PA 02202)
by Ruth Ellinger

GERMAN DANCE, K. 605, No. 3
(PA 02188)
by Wolfgang Amadeus Mozart
arranged by Virginia Speiden Carper

THE HAPPY FARMER AND HIS FAMILY (PA 02321)
by Robert Schumann
arranged by Sylvia Rabinof

POMP AND CIRCUMSTANCE
(PA 02189)
by Edward Elgar
arranged by Virginia Speiden Carper

**ST. ANTHONY CHORALE
(from Brahms' Variations on a Theme by Haydn)**
(PA 02417)
arranged by Virginia Speiden Carper

TRIUMPHAL MARCH (PA 02190)
by Edvard Grieg
arranged by Virginia Speiden Carper

**TWO HANDEL MINUETS
(from "Music for the Royal Fireworks")**
(PA 02416)
by George Frideric Handel
arranged by Virginia Speiden Carper

TWO TRUMPET VOLUNTARIES
(PA 02415)
by Henry Purcell
arranged by Virginia Speiden Carper

**WHEN I AM LAID IN EARTH
(Air, "Dido's Lament")** (PA 02334)
by Henry Purcell
arranged by Sylvia Rabinof